PRINCE
In Small IT Projects

Central Computer and
Telecommunications Agency

LONDON: HMSO

This Practitioner Handbook is part of the PRINCE
Documentation. Project Issue Reports relating to this
handbook should be submitted through the
Departmental PRINCE Co-ordinator to the Secretary of
the PRINCE User Group Change Control Sub Group
for evaluation.

CONTENTS

PRINCE
In Small IT Projects

1 Introduction

1.1 The Handbooks

This booklet is one of a series of PRINCE Practitioner Handbooks designed to supplement the main PRINCE manuals and to assist with the application of PRINCE to specific types of project.

The PRINCE manuals give advice on project management standards, and relate those management standards to a set of technical standards. This handbook is not intended to replace the need for education and training in the techniques, any need for consultancy support, nor other PRINCE documentation. The contents are intended to assist the trained PRINCE practitioner to customise the standards to meet the particular needs of the project in hand. The application of this handbook to a particular project should be agreed in advance with your local PRINCE Co-ordinator.

A list of titles of handbooks it is expected to issue is given in Annex B.

1.2 Scope and purpose of this handbook

People sometimes question whether the PRINCE project management method is appropriate for small projects. They feel instinctively that small projects should be manageable with little effort (which is not always true), or with little being written down (which is seldom, if ever, true). However, even when the need for some formality is accepted and prospective users attempt to adapt PRINCE, it presents such a close-knit set of procedures that it is difficult to separate what is essential from what is merely important.

This handbook is designed to assist with the management of small projects. It shows how the principles of the PRINCE project management standard may be adapted to suit the size, or the cost, of the project involved, by selecting from or varying its procedures to the extent necessary to suit the project's needs for management. It is not a "small projects" version of PRINCE. **There is nothing in the PRINCE method which can be omitted without some loss of control over the project.** What the handbook does is to suggest where, if it is **necessary** to reduce the amount of time to be spent planning and controlling the project, reductions may be made without destroying the fabric of PRINCE and without compromising its principles. But these reductions involve additional risk, and there may be penalties. The guiding principle must be to exclude only what you can afford not to have.

The handbook is complementary to PRINCE, SSADM, and SDM documentation. It assumes that the approach to the project will be as addressed by CCTA's IS Guides, for example on Turnkey projects, the Feasibility Study, or the Full Study. It complements the CCTA IS Guide D1 on Small Systems but additionally relates to all small projects rather than just to those procurements whose estimated value falls below the EC/GATT financial threshold. For more detailed guidance on the application of PRINCE to a particular type of project the reader is referred to the practitioner handbook covering that type of project (See Annex B).

This handbook gives guidelines on the adaptation of the PRINCE standard so that the management burden is not out of proportion to the size or to the cost of the project. At the same time it still retains the management principles and good practices embodied in the standard. It is not intended that for one project these guidelines should apply, whilst for another, slightly larger, project the full PRINCE procedures should apply. There should be a gradual increase in the procedures used to suit the size of the project. **The customisation of PRINCE to specific projects is a matter for the trained practitioner.**

Table 1 opposite indicates the kind of project that would fall into the category anticipated by this handbook. It should be taken as indicative, not as rules to be followed rigidly, without thought for their applicability.

When considering the size of a project, it is wise also to consider whether a number of projects can be grouped together, so that a trained person can be made available to all of them (eg a common PAT).

This handbook assumes a basic knowledge of PRINCE and of the associated terminology.

Project size	Trained staff* available	Action
Less than 9 person months of effort	None	Apply the PRINCE principles of quality control in all projects, and the concepts and principles of planning using a product breakdown structure as appropriate. Do not use the remainder of PRINCE.
Less than 9 person months of effort	Some already in the team	Use common sense to relate the use of PRINCE to the amount of training.
9 person months or more		Follow the guidelines in this handbook.

* People who have attended the full PRINCE Project Organisation, Planning and Control (POPC) course or equivalent — see section 2.5

Table 1: Use of PRINCE with projects of various sizes

2 Organisation

If the project is to be completed successfully, there is need for the demand side and of the supply side to be represented. The representatives will be the Project Board and the Project Manager, respectively. The latter will probably need project teams to help with the work, and this in turn will lead to the need for the monitoring and control procedures referred to in chapter 4.

2.1 Project Board

A Project Board should always be appointed by Senior Management in order to demonstrate their commitment to the project, to allocate and control the use of resources, approve timescales, and be aware of deviations from those factors at exception situations.

The responsibilities outlined in the PRINCE Management Guide should be allocated to the Project Board members. However, it is expected that in most cases there may be only two members of the Project Board, representing between them the Executive, User, and Technical interests in the project. It is suggested that the Executive and Senior User are most appropriate for combination, and that only in the case of hardware procurement will the Senior User and Senior Technical responsibilities be compatible and suitable for combination. **Under no circumstances can the Project Board be reduced to one member.**

The grade of the members of the Project Board should be adjusted to suit the size and/or status of the project.

An alternative solution is to have one Project Board responsible for several small projects. However, care must be taken that the projects **are** related and that the members of the Board are not attending lengthy meetings in which they have only a small interest. This will be particularly true for the Senior User(s) on the Board.

2.2 Project and Stage Managers

It is expected that for most small projects the same individual will take the role of both Project Manager, and Stage Manager for all stages. The time spent will vary according to the size of the project. As with the Project Board, consideration should be given to appointing one person to manage several projects.

Care should be taken that this does not give rise to conflicts of interest or competition for time from several urgent projects.

As the size of the small project approaches that associated with the normal PRINCE procedures it should be considered whether a different Stage Manager should be appointed for different stages.

As with larger projects there is no preset standard by which Project Managers or Stage Managers are selected. Consideration must be given to the type of work and the resource usage in any particular stage before deciding upon the most appropriate individual, whether from a user or a technical area.

2.3   Project Support Office

Ideally there will be a project support office in existence which will

- provide assistance in planning the project

- monitor progress on behalf of the project board and the project manager, in terms of resource allocation and timescales, and deviations which lead to exception situations

- provide an independent quality assurance function; and

- provide an experienced and independent sounding board for the project board and project managers.

This project support office should also fill the roles of the Technical and Business Assurance Co-ordinators for all small projects, and so obviate the need to find resources from an already small team.

2.4   Project Assurance Team

Where no project support office exists, it is necessary to consider whether the tasks in the previous section can be performed elsewhere, for example by a separate quality assurance branch. If they cannot, then the responsibilities outlined in the PRINCE Management Guide should be allocated to a Project Assurance Team (PAT). As with the Project Board, it is expected that in most cases there may be only two members of the PAT representing between them the Business, User, and Technical interests in the project. Again, the Business and User responsibilities are most appropriate for combination; only in the case of a hardware procurement will the User and Technical responsibilities be compatible and suitable for combination. **Under no circumstances should the PAT be reduced to one member.**

It is emphasised that for most projects it will not be necessary to employ individuals full time as members of the PAT. The actual work involved will vary depending upon the responsibility within the PAT, the size of the project in terms of activities and/or resources, and the complexity of the project. It is difficult to quantify the amount of work that will be involved for these reasons although the figures in table 2 may be used as a very general guide to the total effort required for the project, including that element of Project Management and Quality Assurance normally assigned to the PAT.

The grade of the members of the PAT should be adjusted to suit the size and/or status of the project.

Total Effort	person months				
	10	**8–40**	**15–60**	**20–80**	**40–120**
Business Assurance	1	2–3	2–4	3–6	4–8
Technical Assurance	0.5	1–2	2	2	3–4
User Assurance	0.5	1	2	2–3	3–4

Table 2: These figures provide a general guide to the effort required of the Project Assurance Team. They include the elements of project management and quality assurance normally assigned to the PAT.

2.5 Training

The training cost associated with a project should be commensurate with the size of the project. The type of training available, in ascending order of cost, is as follows:

- an overview presentation by either the local PRINCE Co-ordinator, a member of CCTA, or by the Civil Service College, on site or at the College, lasting between 2 hours and one day

- an on-site Team Course, lasting two days, run by either the local PRINCE Co-ordinator, the Civil Service College, or a private sector organisation

- a Project Organisation, Planning, and Control (POPC) Course run by the Civil Service College at Sunningdale or other residential locations, lasting five days, or the private sector equivalent.

Project Board members should receive the Overview. Project Managers and Stage Managers should attend at least the Team Course, but consideration should be given to the POPC course depending upon the size of the project and the likely involvement of the people in future projects. The Business and Technical Assurance Co-ordinators should attend either the Team Course of the POPC Course depending upon the size of the project. The User Assurance Co-ordinator should attend either the Overview or the Team Course depending upon the size of the project.

A minimum of one person on every project should have attended the POPC course or its equivalent. In general, however, the wider view should be encouraged that this training is management training for the future and that the management aspects of the course have a general application.

3   Planning

There is clearly a need for a **product**, since there would not otherwise be a **project**. This product will usually have a number of components, and/or intermediate products. When the product(s) needed have been identified by means of a product breakdown structure, a plan will be needed to set out, at the very least, WHAT is to be produced, WHEN and BY WHOM; and HOW quality is to be specified and measured.

3.1   Project Plans

All projects are established on the basis of what products are needed, and what activities have to be performed by which people. The project must have the aim of producing the required products to an agreed standard of quality, within an agreed timescale and to an approved budget. Therefore the information will exist to construct formal Project Technical and Resource Plans for all projects.

However, it may not be necessary for the smaller projects to produce separate Project Technical and Project Resource Plans. Since the very size of the project will restrict the number of major activities, the planner should aim to accommodate both plans on one A4 sheet. As the projects become larger, consideration should be given to whether this still remains feasible or advisable for the sake of clarity.

3.2   Stage Plans

All projects will be sub-divided into a minimum of two stages, one representing the planning stage, the other the action stage. In the smallest projects the planning stage will represent the initiation of the project when the products are defined, planned, and the organisation and controls appropriate to the size of the project are established. The action stage will then represent the technical development of the project products. With larger projects, consideration should be given to increasing the number of planning and/or action stages.

The number of stages will depend upon the size and type of project. Each will end at a natural breakpoint in the project where **key decisions have to be taken,** and/or where **critical work has to be completed** before the project is allowed to progress further. Although difficult to quantify, smaller projects would not be expectcd to have stages lasting more than two or three elapsed months. As a broad outline, table 3 illustrates some of the factors affecting the staging of a project.

Timescale (elapsed months)	1–6	4–14	8–18	10–20	14–24
Stages	2	3	4	5	6
Effort (man months)	10	8–40	15–60	20–80	40–120

Table 3: These figures provide a general guide to the number of stages appropriate to various sizes of project.

Stage Plans will be necessary for most projects. However it is unlikely that the number of major activities in a small project lasting up to 3 months in elapsed time, or having only two stages, will be sufficient to warrant separate Stage Technical and Stage Resource Plans. In such cases the Project Plans should show sufficient detail to enable control to be exercised over the project on a weekly basis, and Stage Plans need not be constructed provided the Project Board agrees. However for projects of longer duration or increased complexity, Stage Technical and Stage Resource Plans must be constructed.

3.3 **Detailed and Individual Plans**

The need for Detailed or Individual Work Plans is a matter for consideration by the Stage Manager. If the project is complex, or the number of people involved is large, then there may be a case for the construction of such plans. However it is expected that most small projects will find such plans unnecessary.

3.4 **Exception Plans**

Wherever plans exist and controls are used to monitor progress against those plans, procedures must also exist to cater for deviations from those plans. The PRINCE Exception Plan procedures should be used for all small projects.

It is worth emphasising that there is a danger that the amount of effort expended on exception planning will exceed the actual work on the project. For this reason the amount of tolerance[1] should be generous enough to control the frequency of Exception Plan situations, bearing in mind the size of the project and the cost of those procedures.

---

[1] The amount by which the Project Manager/Stage Manager may deviate from the permitted cost or time without the need to refer to the Project Board.

4 Controls

Even in small projects there will be times when what actually happens differs from the plans, and people will want (or need) to make changes. There will thus be need for progress reporting to find out what is happening; for change control procedures of sufficient rigidity (or flexibility) to control those changes so that what is eventually produced is what was required; and for meetings at which the project board can formally ratify decisions.

4.1 Checkpoint Meetings

Checkpoint Meetings will be held for all projects. They provide the means of control on progress and a forum for the identification of problems likely to arise in the future. The frequency of checkpoint meetings for small projects should be determined in the same way as for any other project. They may not need to be so frequent where the members of the project team all sit in the same office. Where the project team is widely distributed there may be a case for holding checkpoint meetings by telephone or in writing in order to save travelling costs.

4.2 Highlight Reports

Highlight Reports should be prepared for all projects based upon the findings at Checkpoint Meetings. The frequency of such reports should be at the discretion of the Project Board but it would be inadvisable to have them less frequently than monthly. Two weeks would be normal. With the Project Board's approval, the Highlight Report could act as a substitute for some of the Project Board meetings, particularly a Mid Stage Assessment (but see 4.3 and 4.4 below).

4.3 End Stage Assessment Meetings

End Stage Assessment (ESA) meetings of the Project Board must be held where the stage was of sufficient duration or criticality. An ESA should be held at the end of the Initiation Stage to confirm the definition of the project in terms of plans and objectives, and to accept the Project Initiation Document. This will normally be combined with the Initiation Meeting. The Project Board must also meet at the end of every project to confirm its satisfactory completion.

Where other stages are of less than six weeks duration then the Project Board may decide to accept a

Highlight Report rather than to have a formal meeting. This is particularly likely when the project management and the teams are a compact unit where contact is easy and frequent.

Whether a meeting is held or not, the members of the Board will always be expected to complete an Approval to Proceed letter authorising progress to the next stage. This should be prepared by the Project Manager and submitted to the Project Board for signature.

4.4	**Mid-Stage Assessment Meetings**	Mid-Stage Assessment Meetings of the Project Board must be held when an Exception Situation has occurred. All other MSA's are at the discretion of the Project Board. Although there is no real substitute for a meeting (which, properly conducted, should be short and constitute very little overhead on the project) it is probable that the approval to proceed with overlapping stages of the smaller project can be satisfied by a written report. However, the members of the Board will always be expected to complete an Approval to Proceed letter. This should be prepared by the Project Manager and submitted to the Project Board for signature. Updating on progress may be satisfied by the Highlight Reports.
4.5	**Quality Reviews**	**All products must have a quality review.** However, there is discretion to involve the minimum number of reviewers necessary to ensure the correctness of the product. This may range from one reviewer, where the product is sufficiently specialised in a user or technical area, to a team of reviewers where the product has a general applicability. The choice of formal or informal review procedures will depend upon the criticality of the product and should be the subject of a recommendation by the Project Manager to the Project Board, made in consultation with the PAT during the preparation for the stage. The extent and type of review should be approved by the Project Board at the same time as it approves stage plans or, where no such plans exist, at the beginning of the project.
4.6	**Change Control Procedures**	In any project that has been planned it will be necessary to control proposals to implement any

changes. It is therefore important that the PRINCE Project Issue Report (Change Control) procedures are **used in all projects.** However, there may be cases where the application of those procedures in full would be excessive in view of the size of the project. To a large extent the flexibility is inherent in the degree of tolerance allowed to the Project Manager, within which changes may be absorbed without prior approval by the Project Board. However, if desired, the Senior User's responsibility for allocating priority to Requests for Change may be delegated to the User Assurance Co-ordinator in smaller projects.

Annex A   Checklists

Management organisation	Project Board (Min 2 members)	Essential
	Project/stage managers	Essential
	Project Assurance Team (Min 2 members)	Essential
	Role description	Essential
	Training	Variable
Planning the project	Project objectives	Essential
	Product Breakdown Structure	Essential
	Project technical plan	Essential
	Project resource plan	Essential
	Stage technical plan	Optional
	Stage resource plan	Optional
	Detailed plan	Optional
	No. of stages (Min of 2)	Variable
	Project Initiation Document	Essential
	Product Description	Variable
Controlling the project	Checkpoint meetings	Essential
	Highlight reports	Essential
	Quality reviews	Essential
	Informal reviews	Variable
	Tolerance	Essential
	Exception plans	Essential
	Mid stage assessment meetings	Optional
	End stage assessment meetings	Essential
	Project Issue Reports	Variable
	Technical exception reports	Variable